THE BERLIN AIRLIFT

Breaking the Soviet Blockade

by Michael Burgan

SNAPSHOTS IN HISTORY

THE BERLIN AIRLIFT

Breaking the Soviet Blockade

by Michael Burgan

Content Adviser: Tom Lansford, Ph.D., Assistant Dean and
Associate Professor of Political Science, College of Arts and Letters,
University of Southern Mississippi

Reading Adviser: Susan Kesselring, M.A., Literacy Educator,
Rosemount-Apple Valley-Eagan (Minnesota) School District

Compass Point Books ✦ Minneapolis, Minnesota

COMPASS POINT BOOKS

3109 West 50th Street, #115
Minneapolis, MN 55410

For Compass Point Books
Brenda Haugen, XNR Productions, Inc., Catherine Neitge,
Keith Griffin, Lori Bye, and Nick Healy

Produced by White-Thomson Publishing Ltd.

For White-Thomson Publishing
Stephen White-Thomson, Susan Crean, Amy Sparks,
Tinstar Design Ltd., Tom Lansford, Peggy Bresnick Kendler,
Barbara Bakowski, and Timothy Griffin

Library of Congress Cataloging-in-Publication Data
Burgan, Michael.
  The berlin airlift: breaking the Soviet blockade / by Michael Burgan.
      p. cm. — (Snapshots in history)
  Includes bibliographical references and index.
  ISBN 978-0-7565-3486-8 (library binding)
1. Berlin (Germany)—History—Blockade, 1948–1949—Juvenile
literature. I. Title. II. Series.
  DD881.B734 2008
  943′.1550874—dc22   2007032697

Visit Compass Point Books on the Internet at
www.compasspointbooks.com
or e-mail your request to
custserv@compasspointbooks.com

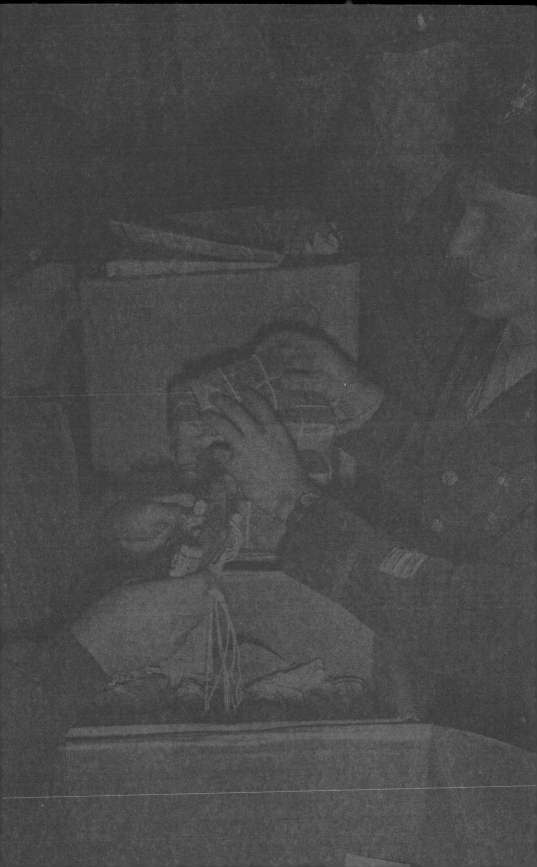

Contents

Hope for the New Year

Christmas 1948 was a bleak time for 16-year-old Karin Kraus. Like most of the other 2.25 million residents of West Berlin, Germany, she ate powdered milk and eggs day after day. Just several miles away, in East Berlin, the residents enjoyed fresh vegetables and real eggs with their holiday meals. But Karin and most other West Berliners refused to shop in the east, where the Soviet Union controlled the government.

Six months earlier, the Soviets had placed a blockade around West Berlin. No goods could enter that half of the city by rail, road, or water. Only one thing kept Karin and the citizens of West Berlin alive: a never-ending airlift. U.S. and British planes made round-the-clock flights into the city, carrying food, coal, medical supplies, and other goods. To Karin and the other residents

During the Berlin Airlift, U.S. and British planes landed in Berlin day and night, while Berliners eagerly awaited the food they carried.

9

of West Berlin, the planes were *Rosinen* bombers, or "raisin bombers." Instead of dropping bombs, the planes brought in raisins and other food.

In November 1948, Europe faced one of its longest stretches of heavy fog ever, lasting for days at a time. William Tunner was the U.S. general in charge of the airlift. He described a "pea-soup fog" on November 30 that was so thick, "you couldn't drive a car in the city that day, much less land a plane." Of the 42 planes that took off for West Berlin on November 30, just one landed there. The others returned to their bases.

GERMANY'S ZONES AND BERLIN'S SECTORS

After World War II, Germany was divided into four zones. The United States, the Soviet Union, Great Britain, and France each controlled one zone. Berlin, the capital of Germany, was located in the Soviet zone. That city was also split among the nations, into four sectors. By blockading the three western sectors, Soviet leader Joseph Stalin hoped to drive the other nations from Berlin. U.S. President Harry S. Truman was just as determined to stay. He wanted to keep democracy in West Berlin.

Because of the bad weather, the city's supplies of coal grew dangerously low. Coal was particularly important because West Berliners relied on it to heat their homes and cook their meager meals. For light, most West Berliners used candles, since electricity was rationed. In East Berlin, the Soviets controlled the power plants that provided most of the electricity for West Berlin. The Soviets had shut down power to the west when they started the blockade. Around Christmastime 1948, Karin Kraus struggled to study for school:

We were running out of candles and the electricity was only on for two hours in the middle of the night. I began a schedule of napping in the late afternoon, getting up to read my schoolbook from two to four in the morning, and then going back to bed so that I could get up at seven to get ready for school.

The winter of 1948 was a harsh one for the people living among Berlin's ruins.

11

An "Operation Santa Claus" plane landed in Berlin in late December 1948, filled with packages of clothing, candy, and toys for children in Berlin.

Even when not fighting the fog, U.S. pilots faced other problems. Soviet fighter planes sometimes flew close by, trying to distract the Americans. Other times, the Soviets directed bright lights into their eyes. Ice on the planes was another danger. Early in the winter of 1948–1949, Howard Myers was flying over East Germany on his way to West Berlin. The ice fouled up one of his engines, and the

plane began to lose altitude. Myers ordered his co-pilot to dump some of the cargo so that the plane could regain height. The plan worked, and Myers landed safely. But later he wondered:

> *What people on the ground in Soviet-controlled East Germany must have thought as over 4,000 pounds [8,800 kilograms] of macaroni came raining out of the sky on that cold winter night.*

When Christmas Day came in 1948, it was just another day at work for the American troops in western Germany and West Berlin. But during the holiday season, they were cheered by the arrival of entertainers from the United States. The practice of sending singers, comedians, and dancers overseas to military bases had begun during World War II. The entertainers sent to Berlin in 1948 included the comedian Bob Hope and songwriter Irving Berlin, who wrote a new song called "Operation Vittles" just for the troops taking part in the airlift. The U.S. government also created "Project Sleighbells," a special airlift that brought the soldiers gifts from their families in the United States.

A GREAT ENTERTAINER

Irving Berlin (1888–1989) came to the United States from Russia in 1893. His hit songs included "God Bless America" and the classic "White Christmas." For the airlift, the songwriter took an existing tune and added new words, such as, "Thanks to the fighting Air Force/ That daily took its toll;/ Now it's a humane Air Force/ With heart and soul,/ Dropping wheat and coal." He also joked that he was changing his last name to Jones, because "Anything over here named Berlin, they cut up into sectors!" The troops in the audience gave him a round of applause for his wit and his song.

For the Christmas holiday, U.S. troops made an extra effort to help the West Germans who lived near them. Navy fliers stationed in Frankfurt donated clothing, food, toys, and candy to orphaned children. West Berliners also received gifts. And on December 26, the planes managed to bring in more than 6,000 tons (5,400 metric tons) of supplies—the third-highest single-day total since the start of the airlift in June.

A group of U.S fliers bought Clarence the Camel for $24, then took him to Berlin.

14

A CHRISTMAS CAMEL

During the 1948 holiday season, one plane reached Berlin with an unusual passenger: Clarence the Camel. While serving in North Africa, U.S. pilots had bought the young camel. He served as a mascot for a flight crew. The pilots thought that Clarence would cheer up the children of Berlin. The first Clarence was injured before making the flight, so the Americans went back to North Africa and bought a second camel. This one was also called Clarence, even though "he" was actually a "she." Clarence arrived in Berlin wearing special bags filled with food for the children. When Clarence landed, 5,000 children came out to greet him, leading one disappointed teacher to say, "Only one camel for so many people!" Later Clarence made other trips to Berlin with more gifts.

January 1949 brought new confidence to the officers running the airlift. To show their thanks, some West Berliners put on their best clothes and brought gifts to the Americans working at Tempelhof, the airport in the U.S. sector. A newspaper reported that thousands of the residents flooded the field. The gifts included "small hand-carved toys, old silver, or china salvaged [saved] from the ruins of the city."

The winter weather eased somewhat, and better technology was making it easier to direct the planes. But West Berliners still faced difficult times ahead, and no one knew how long Soviet leader Joseph Stalin would keep his tight grip around the city. Residents like Karin Kraus would face more meals with powdered eggs and more nights of hearing the sounds of planes constantly flying overhead.

War in Europe

Chapter

2

During the first decades of the 20th century, Berliners saw their city rise and fall. Germany was one of the great European powers when World War I began in 1914, and Berlin was its capital. But Germany and its allies lost the war. The victors, especially Great Britain and France, demanded that the Germans pay reparations. This money would cover the costs of the damage Germany had caused during World War I. The reparations totaled about $27 billion.

During the early 1920s, the German economy crumbled. German money, known as marks, became almost worthless. People hauled marks in wheelbarrows just to pay for their daily food. Germany suffered again after 1929, when most of the world entered the Great Depression.

During the 1920s, some Berliners used baskets to carry money to and from the bank.

Companies shut down because people stopped buying many goods. Workers lost their jobs—and sometimes their life's savings.

As Germans struggled to survive, new political parties rose in Germany. They tried to find ways to end the crisis and to restore German pride. The most successful of these parties was the National Socialist Party, or the Nazis. Its leader was Adolf Hitler. He detested the Treaty of Versailles, which ended World War I, because he thought it left Germany weak.

In 1933, Hitler was elected chancellor of Germany, an important government post. He used his power to put the Nazis in charge of Germany. Soon he began to ignore the restrictions that the Treaty of Versailles put on rebuilding the German military. He also began taking over lands in Europe where many Germans lived.

In September 1939, Hitler invaded Poland. This attack launched World War II. Great Britain and France led the effort to help Poland fight the Nazis. The United States hoped to stay out of the war. After World War I, many Americans did not want to get involved in European affairs. The country was still coping with the Great Depression. But on December 7, 1941, Japanese planes attacked U.S. naval ships at Pearl Harbor, Hawaii. The next day, President Franklin Roosevelt asked Congress to declare war on Japan. Soon the Americans were also at war with Japan's allies, Germany and Italy.

By this time, Hitler had taken over most of Western Europe as well as parts of North Africa. German troops had invaded the Soviet Union, too. Many American and British people did not trust Soviet leader Joseph Stalin because of his communist beliefs. But President Roosevelt and British leader Winston Churchill knew they would have to work with Stalin to defeat Nazi Germany. The three Allied leaders became known as the Big Three. They met for the first time in Tehran, Iran, in November 1943. They discussed plans for a massive invasion of France, which was now under German control. They also began to talk about the future of Germany once the war was over. The Big Three left the details of Germany's future to the European Advisory Commission, which they had just formed for that purpose.

A CRUEL ALLY

When he was a young man, Joseph Dzhugashvili (1878–1953) changed his last name to Stalin, Russian for "man of steel." As the leader of the Soviet Union from 1928 to 1953, Stalin proved to be as hard and as cold as that metal. He spied on the Soviet people and killed anyone whom he thought might threaten his rule. His efforts to create a communist society led to the starvation of millions of his own citizens. Stalin believed that communism would one day be the only form of government in the world. The only thing stopping its progress was capitalist countries such as the United States. Stalin wanted to make the Soviet Union powerful enough to defeat the capitalist nations and help the spread of communism.

The Allied invasion of France was called Operation Overlord. It began on June 6, 1944— D-Day. British, Canadian, and American forces, with French help, slowly drove the Germans out of France and its neighboring lands. At the same

PAI3-25

The invasion of France began when more than 1 million Allied troops came ashore on June 6, 1944, known ever since as D-Day.

time, the Soviets were pushing the Nazis westward, out of Eastern Europe. As the fighting went on, the European Advisory Commission met on August 2, 1944, to discuss the future of Germany. It decided:

> *Germany, within her frontiers as they were on the 31st December, 1937, will, for the purposes of occupation, be divided into three zones, one of which will be allotted to each of the three powers, and a special Berlin area, which will be under joint occupation by the three powers.*

In February 1945, Roosevelt, Churchill, and Stalin met again, this time in the Soviet city of Yalta. Roosevelt and Churchill said France should play a role in postwar Germany. They proposed giving the French part of their zones and some control in Berlin as well. Stalin agreed, since the Soviet share of Germany would remain the same. The Big Three also agreed that each zone would have its own military commander. Together, the four commanders would form the Allied Control Council, which would oversee the rebuilding of Germany.

As the Allied leaders talked in Yalta, the fighting continued. By the end of April 1945, the Soviet army was inside Berlin. American troops were in Germany, too, west of Berlin. They controlled land that would become part of the Soviet zone. After the war in Europe ended on May 8, these U.S. forces pulled back so the Soviets could take control. A few months later, the Soviet troops pulled out of the British, American, and French sectors in Berlin.

By the time the Allies defeated Nazi Germany, President Roosevelt had died. Vice President Harry S. Truman had become president. Although World War II was over in Europe, the fighting against Japan continued. In July, Truman traveled to Potsdam, a town just outside Berlin. There he met with Stalin and British leader Clement Attlee. Truman thought that he could get along with Stalin. Later he would angrily remember that Stalin broke many agreements made at Potsdam "as soon as the unconscionable [dishonest] Russian dictator returned to Moscow!"

Stalin wanted Germany to pay reparations. The United States and Great Britain said the Soviets could take reparations only from their own zone. The Americans and the British did, however, agree to let the Soviets take some industrial equipment from the other three zones. In return, the Soviet Union would send food to the other three zones. The victors also agreed to hold democratic elections. The Soviets, however, were already working to put communists in control in their zone.

When the Big Three Allied leaders met at Potsdam, Truman (front right) thought he could trust Stalin (front left). But Stalin soon broke that trust.

As the Potsdam meeting continued, President Truman learned about the successful testing of a new weapon. Deep in the desert of New Mexico, scientists had exploded the first atomic bomb.

In August 1945, the United States dropped two atomic bombs on Japan. Shortly after, the Japanese surrendered. The knowledge to build these nuclear weapons gave the United States the most powerful military in the world. The Soviet Union, however, wanted to challenge U.S. power.

World War II was over, but the Cold War between the United States and the Soviet Union was about to begin. For the most part, the Cold War was a war of ideas rather than direct fighting. Each country tried to spread its influence around the world while weakening its enemy wherever it could.

THE COLD WAR

The term *Cold War* was used in contrast to a "hot" war, which featured armies battling each other for land. During the Cold War, the Soviet Union wanted to promote communism. Under communism, a country's government is controlled by the Communist Party. A communist government owns most businesses and property, and it strictly limits personal freedom. During the Cold War, the United States and the Soviet Union gave money and weapons to countries and groups that supported each of them. The Cold War lasted from 1945 to 1991, the year the Soviet Union collapsed. Today there are 15 nations that were once part of the Soviet Union. Some have democratic governments, while others do not.

23

A Defeated, Divided City

Chapter

3

About 4.6 million people lived in Berlin when World War II began. As the war in Europe ended in May 1945, just 2.8 million remained. Those who were lost included young men in the German military who had died in battle. Others were Jews and so-called political criminals who were sent to special prisons, called concentration camps. The Germans killed more than 7 million people in concentration camps, mostly Jews from Germany and other European nations. Some Berlin residents simply fled the city as it became a target of the Allies. Other Berliners were killed in these attacks.

The people who remained in Berlin were mostly women, the elderly, and children. They had endured several years of bombing by British and U.S. planes. In the last weeks of the war,

Soviet planes roared in from the east. Karin Kraus remembered how they "flew low and fired machine guns at people moving in the streets." Soviet artillery fire soon followed the planes, and then came tanks and soldiers.

By the end of World War II, most of Berlin's buildings were heavily damaged.

When the fighting finally ended, Berlin was in ruins. About 20 percent of all the homes in the city had been destroyed, and most of the ones still standing were damaged. Colonel H.G. Sheen, one of the first Americans to enter Berlin, filed this report:

> *The bomb damage in the heart of the city is hard to describe. In certain areas the stench of unburied dead is almost overpowering. From Tempelhof to the Wilhelmstrasse, not one undamaged building is standing; roofs, floors, and windows are gone; and in many cases the fragments of only one or two walls are standing.*

The war had also ruined the city's economy. Workers were scarce, particularly doctors. Many of them had left the city to serve with the military or had been killed. The Soviets shut all the banks, and no one received government funds they had previously received under the Nazis. Few people had money, but even if they did, shops had almost nothing to sell. As food ran out, some people ate horses. Worst of all, to the Berliners, was the arrival of the Soviet troops. For almost two months, they were the rulers of the city, and they terrorized tens of thousands of Berliners. They threatened to kill any civilians who hid German soldiers in their homes.

Victorious Soviet soldiers often stole from the people they met. Watches were a favorite item. Other Soviets raped German women. Karin Kraus tried to make herself look ugly so the soldiers

THE BLACK MARKET

Berliners desperate for food and other items turned to the black market—"black" because it was not officially approved. People traded extra food they might have for valuables that other Berliners offered, including jewelry, clocks, and cameras. Also valuable were cigarettes and alcohol. In Berlin, cigarettes were used instead of money to buy goods. One carton of cigarettes was worth up to $100, and even the butts of half-smoked cigarettes were collected and traded. U.S. soldiers, who bought the cigarettes cheaply at their military bases, sometimes exchanged them at the black markets. Some soldiers sent home thousands of dollars that they made at the black markets in Berlin.

would leave her alone. She wore tattered old clothes and smeared her face with dirt. When a Soviet soldier approached her, she later wrote, "I walked pigeon-toed, crossed my eyes, and let ... spit dribble down my chin." The soldier fled in horror. But many other women weren't as lucky. Ingeborg Dedering, a Berlin teenager, reported that two women she knew committed suicide because of the Soviets. They "poisoned themselves after they had been mistreated in the worst way by drunken Russian [Soviet] soldiers." Ingeborg hid in a box in her parents' basement to avoid the same kind of mistreatment.

Many Berliners' hopes rose in July 1945 with the arrival of British and U.S. troops. (The French took control of their sector later.) Unlike the Soviets, these forces treated the Germans decently. Many Berliners fled the Soviet sector to live in the other sectors. But groups of Soviet soldiers sometimes wandered into those sectors and committed crimes.

In one incident, Soviet soldiers killed two young girls while robbing them of their watches.

Even without the threat of Soviet crimes, Berliners struggled to survive. Some searched the ground for chestnuts, which they ground into flour to make bread. As cold weather approached, Berliners hunted for wood to heat their homes. They found some in the ruins of buildings. Other wood came from the trees in the city's parks and zoo. Still the winter of 1945 was hard. Ella Barowsky, who lived in the Soviet sector, said, "Old people died of hunger and cold; they died like flies."

As difficult as life was in Berlin, refugees came to the city from Eastern Europe and other parts of Germany. Conditions were even worse in their hometowns, and they hoped they might have better luck surviving in Berlin.

In the British sector of Berlin, hungry women looked for scraps of food or things they could trade on the black market.

Food was scarce across the city—a condition made worse by the Soviets. Before leaving the other sectors of Berlin, the Soviets had stolen 7,000 cows, along with machinery and pipes from buildings. The Soviets also limited access to farms in the Soviet zone outside Berlin. The Soviets wanted the food for their troops in Germany. Still some Berliners managed to reach farms in the countryside.

Colonel Frank Howley was in charge of the American sector. He described the residents' efforts to find food:

> *Berliners, either walking or taking trains to the country, were bringing back on their shoulders, or in shopping bags, 100 tons [90 metric tons] of fresh vegetables every day. This helped feed the city.*

Food that the United States and its allies brought into Berlin was strictly rationed. Some of this food came from the German sectors, but other food was sent from the United States and Great Britain. Age and work status determined how much food a person received. Workers with demanding jobs, such as mining coal, received the most, and adults without jobs received the least. Children received a bit more than nonworking adults, since children need food to grow.

U.S. soldiers had a positive relationship with Berliners. The U.S. troops often hired Berliners to help rebuild the city. Groups of German women cleared bricks from the streets, piling them in huge mounds. The women were soon nicknamed *Trummerfrauen*, or "rubble women." One of the mounds they helped build became the highest spot in Berlin. The workers earned little money, but more important was the one meal the Americans gave them each day.

The Americans also began to spend time with German civilians. Some dated German women, and a few had children with them. In their free time, soldiers also played with German youths and set up clubs for them. The U.S. government set

The "rubble women" of Berlin helped the United States and its allies start to rebuild their sectors of the city.

COLD WAR AIRWAVES

After Berlin was divided, the Soviet Union controlled the only radio station still able to broadcast. The Soviets refused to let the United States and its allies use it, and they aired propaganda promoting Soviet interests. The Americans decided they needed to broadcast accurate news to Berliners, so in February 1946 they opened Radio in the American Sector (RIAS). The station broadcast German and American music as well as news about food rationing and possible jobs. RIAS also broadcast educational programs for both children and adults. Some of these helped teach the Germans about democracy. Berliners trusted RIAS to give them a fair view of current events, compared to the propaganda the Soviets broadcast from their station. RIAS would prove particularly useful during elections and the Berlin Airlift.

up a program called German Youth Activities (GYA). The kids had fun in the GYA clubs, as Helga Mellman recalled:

> *Once a week the Americans came and they supplied us with records. And when we cleaned up, we got peanut butter and Coca-Cola. We had a dancing floor, we had Ping-Pong. ... And all these things were completely new to us. We are a generation which grew up during the war, and we didn't have anything.*

The clubs helped the Americans win the support of the German people. They helped weaken the impact of Soviet propaganda, which tried to make the Soviets and communism look appealing to the defeated Germans. The clubs also were part of U.S. efforts to rid Germany of Nazi ideas. The youths would learn about democracy and other American values. The United States wanted to rebuild Germany as a democratic, capitalist nation

31

that would be friendly with its former enemies. The Soviets, however, had other plans for Berlin and the rest of Germany.

After World War II, Joseph Stalin wanted to make sure Germany and other European nations would not threaten his country again. This thought, along with the desire to spread communism, fueled Soviet actions in Germany after the war. Stalin did not want the four occupied zones in Germany to form a single nation unless he could dominate it. He resisted efforts to reunite the zones as a democratic German state, and he wanted communist control in Berlin as well.

After the war, the ruling body of the four occupying nations in Berlin was called the Kommandatura. Colonel Frank Howley represented the United States in the Kommandatura. He earned the nickname "Howlin' Mad Howley" because he often failed to keep his temper in check when meeting with the Soviets. Howley took orders from General Lucius Clay, the military governor of the U.S. zone. Clay wanted early elections to be held in Berlin so the people could choose their own leaders. The Kommandatura, however, would still hold the final power as long as Berlin was occupied.

The Kommandatura set elections in Berlin for October 1946. In their sector, the Soviets had created a powerful Communist Party called the Sozialistische Einheitspartei Deutschlands (Socialist Unity Party), or SED. But in other parts of

A DEFENDER OF FREEDOM

General Lucius Clay first came to Berlin in May 1945. He served as the top aide to General Dwight D. Eisenhower, who had led the D-Day landing in 1944. In 1947, President Truman named Clay the commander of all U.S. military forces in Europe as well as the governor of the U.S. zone. Until leaving Germany in 1949, Clay tried to end Nazi influence in Germany and spread democratic values. Some historians say he helped build the modern state of Germany. West Berliners remember him for his efforts to keep residents of their city alive during the Soviet blockade of 1948–1949. Clay later returned to Berlin, after the East German government built a wall separating East Berlin from West Berlin. Clay once again inspired hope in the citizens of West Berlin. Clay died in 1978, and Berliners sent a plaque to his gravesite at the U.S. Military Academy at West Point, New York. The plaque calls Clay *dem Bewahrer unserer Freiheit*—"the defender of our freedom."

the city, the communists had few backers. As the election approached, the Soviets tried to win more support in the rest of Berlin. They gave citizens extra food and supplies. Schoolchildren received cakes and notebooks for school. The Soviets also turned to violence, sending thugs to break up the meetings of rival parties.

The Soviets' efforts, however, may have cost the SED as many votes as it won. When the election results were in, the communists won just 20 percent of the seats on the city council. The Social Democrats won almost half the seats, and two other pro-democracy parties won the rest. Ernst Reuter, a Social Democrat, was elected mayor of Berlin. The Soviets, however, refused to let him take power. And in their sector, they placed the SED in charge of local districts.

The political battles were not the major concern of most Berliners. They were still trying to find basic necessities, such as food and comfort. As 1947 began, most of Europe faced one of the worst winters on record. Families went weeks without meat. In school, children received a bit of chocolate every five days. Most ate the candy on the spot so no one would take it from them and sell it on the black market. In Karin Kraus' Berlin home, the water pipes froze and broke. Her family then used melted snow for water. The local newspaper, she later recalled, "printed a daily report of how many people were found frozen in their beds each morning."

The blizzards and freezing temperatures struck Great Britain, too. People there saw their bread rationed because much of the country's grain was being sent to help the Germans. The British economy was still struggling from the war, and the harsh weather made it much worse. The government decided to save money by cutting off some foreign aid. It would stop sending money to Greece and Turkey. In both nations, communists were trying to seize power. The British asked the Americans to replace the aid they could no longer give.

On March 12, 1947, President Truman spoke to Congress. He outlined his plan to send $400 million in aid to Turkey and Greece. He also promised to help other people around the world resist communism. Truman's new policy, which came to be called the Truman Doctrine, reflected the idea of containment. The United States would not fight wars to drive out communists where they already ruled. But the U.S. government would do whatever it could to stop communism from spreading.

As the Truman Doctrine and the Marshall Plan unfolded, the U.S. government remained deeply concerned about the future of Germany. The Soviet Union insisted on more reparations from the Germans, which the United States and its allies resisted. The Soviets also wanted partial control of the Ruhr Valley. This major coal-producing region was in the British zone. Again the United States and its allies refused to concur with the Soviets. By now, the Americans and the British were treating their zones as one united economic area. They called this region Bizonia, with *bi* meaning "two" and *zonia* referring to the zones. The Soviets opposed this union, but they had no legal power to stop it.

THE MARSHALL PLAN

Within a few months of President Truman's aid package to Turkey and Greece, the U.S. government announced a new plan to help fight communism. The plan, named for Secretary of State George Marshall, would offer billions of dollars in aid to European countries. The Americans believed that strong capitalist economies in Europe would turn people away from communism. By September 1947, 16 countries had agreed to take part in the Marshall Plan. Some of this money eventually helped create 150,000 new jobs in the non-Soviet sectors of Berlin.

Starting in January 1948, diplomats from the United States, France, and Great Britain, as well as several other Western European nations, held a series of meetings in London. They decided that the French zone and Bizonia should be combined

Germany After World War II

Berlin was located within the Soviet zone of Germany, but the city itself was split into four sectors occupied by the Allies.

to create one new nation of West Germany. This country would be democratic and have economic ties to the United States and its allies. If they did not take this step, U.S. leaders feared that the Soviets would spread their influence—and communism— through all of Germany. They saw that the Soviet zone was already under communist control. The

Soviets were not invited to the London meetings, but they had spies in London who later reported on the plans.

Fanning the fears of the United States and its allies were events in Czechoslovakia. Since 1946, the country had both communists and non-communists in the government. But in February 1948, pro-Soviet communists took complete power. The country was now behind what British leader Winston Churchill had called the Iron Curtain. This invisible line marked the division between European countries that practiced democracy and European countries that were communist. U.S. leaders and their allies did not want all of Germany to also fall on the Soviet side of the Iron Curtain.

Relations between the United States and the Soviet Union continued to worsen. On March 5, General Clay sent a message to President Truman noting that relations were tense. On March 20, Clay went to a meeting of the Allied Control Council, which was led at the time by Soviet General Vassily Sokolovsky. The general asked Clay and the British representative about the meetings in London. They refused to answer, although Sokolovsky already knew what had happened there, thanks to the Soviet spies. Sokolovsky then took his aides and left the meeting. The council never met again, and tensions in Berlin were about to rise even further.

Trouble Brews in Berlin

Chapter

4

Even before the March 20, 1948, meeting of the Allied Control Council, the Soviet attitude had changed. The Soviets increasingly showed their dislike of the United States and its allies and their ideas. In January and February 1948, the Soviets began seizing—and sometimes burning—newspapers and magazines printed in the other zones and brought into their zone and their sector of Berlin.

The Soviet Union also began to try to limit free travel between the different zones of Germany. By an earlier agreement, the Soviets controlled the country's railways. They began limiting the amount of goods factories could ship to the other zones. They also claimed they had a right to see who rode on passenger trains, including ones run by the British and the Americans.

General Clay put armed soldiers on the trains so Soviet inspectors would not bother the passengers. Even so, the inspectors came on board, and trains sometimes sat on the tracks for hours. On the roads, the Soviets shut down one main bridge crossing the Elbe River in the British zone. They claimed the bridge needed repairs. The British offered to build a new one, but the Soviets said no. They simply wanted to make traveling as difficult as possible for the United States and its allies. Their actions frightened some Berliners, such as Alice Sawadda. She later recalled, "We felt very scared that the Russians would take us again."

Soviet-controlled German police checked German trucks on their way into the British sector of Berlin.

In response to the Soviet blockade, a barrier was placed between the American and Soviet sectors.

The United States and its allies did not have any legal guarantee to use the roads and railways through the Soviet zone into their sectors of Berlin. The Soviets used this fact to hurt their enemies. On April 1, 1948, the Soviets announced even tighter restrictions on rail and road travel into Berlin. From then on, the Soviet commander in the city had to approve the shipping of all cargo by rail. Passenger trains were later included in this order.

Stalin hoped his actions would drive the United States and its allies out of Berlin. But he was not willing to fight over the city. The Soviet Union had suffered terrible losses during World War II, and Stalin was not prepared to fight another major war. And he did not have a weapon to match the Americans' atomic bomb. Even so, he would put as much pressure on the United States and its allies as he could to try to get them out of Berlin.

To defy Stalin, General Clay once again wanted to put armed soldiers on the trains. This time, U.S. officials in Washington, D.C., said no. He then saw just one way to get supplies into Berlin—by air. By diplomatic agreement, the United States and its allies were allowed to fly their planes along three corridors over the Soviet zone of Germany. The corridors, each 20 miles (32 kilometers) wide, started at air bases in Hamburg and Buckeburg, in the British zone, and Frankfurt, in the U.S. zone. They ended at Tempelhof and Gatow airports in West Berlin.

On April 2, Clay put General Curtis LeMay in charge of what became known as the Little Lift. C-47 Skytrain cargo planes began bringing in supplies for military troops in Berlin. The planes carried

MASTERS OF THE SKIES

After World War II, General Dwight D. Eisenhower called the C-47 Skytrain one of the two most important weapons of the war—the other was the jeep. Built by the Douglas Aircraft Company, the two-engine plane was nicknamed the "Gooney Bird." It was originally designed to carry passengers. When the war began, Douglas equipped the plane to carry up to 3 tons (2.7 metric tons) of cargo. One type of C-47 was used to drop paratroopers into battle. Douglas also built the C-54 Skymaster, which had four engines and room for 49 passengers. President Roosevelt had his own special Skymaster that he used for foreign trips. The C-54 also carried cargo, and during the Berlin Airlift it carried more tonnage than any other plane. General William Tunner called the C-54 "the best ... and a joy to every pilot who ever flew one."

41

extra coal and food so the military could build a stockpile of these essential items. Dakotas, British planes similar to the C-47, also took part.

For West Berliners, the restrictions on travel affected their ability to get to work or visit relatives in the Soviet sector. They also faced dangers. Soviet spies and Germans working for them sometimes picked up Berliners off the streets in the western sectors. They claimed the Germans were wanted for crimes. Many were people who had opposed communist influence in East Berlin. Even people who were not kidnapped feared for their safety. Karin Hueckstaedt lived in Berlin at the time. She remembered, "They [the communists] tried to coerce [force] the people that lived in the west to side with them, with their regime [government]."

During the next two months, the Soviets kept increasing their restrictions on travel. They stopped barges from sailing on rivers, claiming that captains lacked the correct

Danger in the Air

The deadliest moment of the Little Lift came in April 1948. As a British civilian plane came down to land in Berlin, a Soviet Yak fighter jet flew nearby. The fighter passed close to the British plane, making it hard for the pilot to land. When the Yak came by a second time, it collided with the passenger plane, killing 14 people on board. U.S. and British officials reacted angrily, and they made plans to have their own fighter jets offer protection to transport planes coming into Berlin. The Soviets replied that the collision was an accident and that their planes would not bother U.S. and British aircraft. But when the main airlift began, Soviet planes continued to disturb transports flying in the air corridors to Berlin.

paperwork. The Soviets stopped trains carrying coal and mail, which they said did not have proper permission. All road traffic was searched, and so were all passenger trains. By June 19, all passenger train service was halted, supposedly because of damaged tracks. Berliners, however, knew better. The Soviets were simply trying to tighten their grip on Berlin.

Another big conflict in Berlin came over money. The United States and its allies had been talking for months about introducing a new currency, the deutsche mark. The new currency would make the old money earned by the black marketers worthless. The leaders wanted to end the black markets and have greater control over the economy in Berlin.

The United States and its allies announced they would begin using the deutsche mark in their zones. On June 22, the four occupying powers met to discuss a new currency for Berlin as well. The Soviets wanted to control all the money used in Berlin, but the United States and its allies wanted to use the deutsche mark. They had already secretly brought 10 planeloads of the currency into the city and stamped it with a *B*, for Berlin. Karin Kraus remembered her grandmother's thoughts on the argument over the currency:

> *If the Russians could have had their way ... [they] would have controlled our economy. My God, we could have been another Poland or Hungary, all under Soviet rule.*

During the next few days, new B-marks were handed out in West Berlin, while the Soviets introduced a new ostmark in their sector. The Soviets wanted ostmarks used throughout all the sectors instead of the B-marks. Any East Berliner caught using B-marks would be arrested as "an enemy of the German economy."

On June 23, the Berlin city council met to discuss the two currencies. The meeting hall was in the Soviet sector, and communists attacked some non-communists who suggested that both marks be used in the city. Communist police stood by without stopping the violence. In the end, the council voted to use the B-marks in West Berlin and the ostmarks in East Berlin.

Starting in June 1948, new deutsche marks were used in West Berlin.

This decision conflicted with the Soviets' wish to prevent the use of the B-marks anywhere in Berlin. Marshal Sokolovsky contacted officials in

44

Moscow for orders. The Soviet general asked if he should bring tanks into the city. On the other end, Soviet Foreign Minister Vyacheslav Molotov said:

> *No, don't do that. Let's wait a bit. If you bring in the tanks you will be accused of planning to seize the whole of Berlin and they will bring out their tanks. It's better to resolve this issue by using diplomatic language.*

But Molotov and Stalin did not want to talk with the Western nations. They felt actions would speak louder than words. The restrictions on travel into Berlin would now become a full-blown blockade.

The Airlift Begins

Chapter 5

On June 24, 1948, Karin Kraus and her family were eating their morning oatmeal when they learned their lives were about to change. A radio newscast reported that during the night, the Soviets had begun a total blockade of the western sectors of Berlin. All railways were shut down, and soon the roads and waterways would be closed as well. The Soviets also turned off the power plants in their sector that provided electricity to West Berlin.

General Clay thought that a convoy of trucks guarded by troops could carry supplies through the Soviet zone of Germany and then into Berlin. He knew that this move could risk fighting between the Americans and the Soviets. Soviet troops outnumbered the Western allies by eight to one. Still Clay was ready to challenge the Soviets.

German police and American soldiers in West Berlin faced Soviet soldiers in East Berlin during the standoff in 1948.

YOU ARE LEAVING
THE AMERICAN SECTOR
ВЫ ВЫЕЗЖАЕТЕ ИЗ
АМЕРИКАНСКОЙ ЗОНЫ
VOUS SORTEZ
DU SECTEUR AMERICAIN

While waiting for word from Washington on his plan, Clay ordered General LeMay to get every cargo plane possible to Germany. Clay wanted to turn the Little Lift into a larger airlift. But even he doubted the airlift could bring in enough supplies for 2.25 million West Berliners. The city would need about 4,500 tons (4,082 metric tons) of supplies every day, including 1,500 tons (1,361 metric tons) of food. The city had only enough food on hand to last for 36 days, and its coal supplies would run out in about six weeks.

Clay soon met with Ernst Reuter, the mayor of Berlin. Clay outlined the situation:

> *No matter what we do, Berliners are going to be short of fuel and short of electricity. ... There will be times when they are going to be very cold and miserable. Unless they are willing to take this and stay with us, we can't run this.*

Reuter told the general, "I do assure you, the Berliners will take it." Reuter knew Berliners would put up with any problem to avoid Soviet rule.

President Truman would not risk a direct conflict with the Soviets, so planes, not trucks, would have to supply Berlin. The Berlin Airlift officially began on June 26, 1948. The first planes to land were C-47s carrying 80 tons (72 metric tons) of food, medicine, and other supplies. Within two days, the planes were bringing in almost 400 tons (360 metric tons), and the tonnage kept rising as more planes took part.

A C-47 landed at Tempelhof Airport every eight minutes, with German civilians waiting to unload the cargo. The British also flew in goods using their Dakotas, as well as other cargo planes and seaplanes, which landed on West Berlin's Lake Wannsee. The British called their part of the airlift Operation Plainfare. The Americans called their efforts Operation Vittles, after the American slang word for food.

Germans too young to help with the airlift watched the nonstop action. Eberhard Diepgen lived near Gatow Airport, in the British sector. As an adult, he became the mayor of Berlin. He learned to tell the difference between the various planes and watched the British seaplanes land. "Of course, we schoolboys were fascinated by this spectacle."

Standing on rubble from a bombed-out building, young Berliners greeted a U.S. cargo plane bringing supplies to their city.

49

Some of the American troops nicknamed the airlift "LeMay's Coal and Feed Delivery Service." Coal was especially important for Berlin. It was needed to provide power and heat. The city's water system used coal-powered pumps to send water to homes. When the blockade was announced, women in the western sectors filled their bathtubs and buckets with water, in case the supply ran out. Berlin's sewage treatment plants also ran on coal. City officials decided they would have to dump raw sewage into the canals and rivers to save coal.

Most of Berlin's coal came from the western zones of Germany. Transporting coal in planes was hard. The black coal dust filled the planes

General Curtis LeMay, who served in the U.S. military for almost 40 years, reviewed air routes around the globe.

and fouled up sensitive equipment. Crewmembers complained that the dust made it hard for them to breathe and gave them headaches. One pilot recalled flying with the escape hatch open so the dust would be sucked out of the plane. At first the Americans stuffed coal inside duffel bags, the cloth bags soldiers used to carry their gear. Later they developed special paper bags that would hold in coal dust.

As they carried out the airlift, the United States and its allies responded to the Soviet blockade with a counter-blockade of their own. They refused to send food and medicine to the Soviet sector, and they shut down railways from their zones into the Soviet zone. The Soviets soon wrestled with their own shortage of coal and other supplies, and German factories in their zone could not ship out their products because of the counter-blockade.

Even with the two blockades in place, Berlin was not a divided city. Tens of thousands of Berliners crossed from one sector to another to work. Some managed to sneak food into the western sectors and sell it on the black market, which was still in operation. And some West Berliners were tempted by the food and other comforts available in the Soviet sector. Berlin resident Heinz Weber recalled:

> *If you wanted to go out, you had to go into the eastern sector. There were dance halls, there was music, there was electric lighting. The rooms were heated and normal peacetime conditions prevailed.*

Only about 10 percent of West Berlin's 2.25 million residents went into East Berlin to get food. The other 90 percent despised the Soviets and communism so much, they would rather go hungry. To get more food, people planted vegetable gardens wherever they could, even along busy streets.

Within days of starting the airlift, Clay asked for C-54 Skymasters to help carry cargo. Each one could haul three times as much as a C-47. The British suggested that the United States send B-29 bombers to Europe as well. Two of these planes had been used to drop atomic bombs on Japan at the end of the war. The Western allies hoped the bombers' presence in Europe would show Stalin that they were serious about ending the blockade. But at the same time, U.S. officials hoped talks would end the crisis. No one wanted to fight another war in Europe.

By July 30, 1948, the amount of supplies reaching Berlin was almost 2,000 tons (1,800 metric tons) per day. By now, the Berliners were calling this effort the *Luftbrucke*, or "air bridge." The tonnage kept rising as more C-54 Skymasters joined the airlift and crews flew more flights each day. The planes also carried less of their own fuel so they could carry more cargo on each flight.

The constant flights, however, created problems at Tempelhof. The single runway was not strong enough to withstand the landing of so many heavy planes. German civilians, men and women, were hired to fix the runway. They worked quickly between the arrivals and departures of the planes. Two new runways, made from the rubble of Berlin's damaged buildings, were built before the end of the summer.

Although General LeMay had some success with the airlift, his training was in combat. U.S. officials decided to bring in an expert to run the Berlin operation. General William Tunner had run a massive airlift supplying Allied troops in China during World War II. Tunner believed that a successful airlift operation was "about as glamorous as drops of water on a stone. There's no frenzy, no flap, just the inexorable [constant] process of getting the job done." He arrived in Berlin on July 28 and worked to get even more planes into Berlin.

Crews quickly unloaded C-47 Skytrains at Tempelhof Airport.

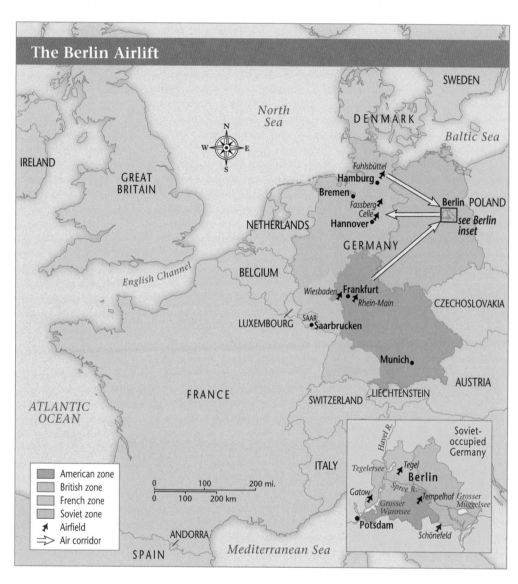

The Berlin Airlift

SWEDEN

North Sea

DENMARK

Baltic Sea

IRELAND

GREAT BRITAIN

Fuhlsbüttel

Hamburg

Bremen

Fassberg
Celle

Hannover

NETHERLANDS

Berlin POLAND

see Berlin inset

GERMANY

BELGIUM

English Channel

Wiesbaden Frankfurt

Rhein-Main

CZECHOSLOVAKIA

LUXEMBOURG

SAAR
•Saarbrucken

Munich

AUSTRIA

FRANCE

SWITZERLAND LIECHTENSTEIN

ATLANTIC OCEAN

Soviet-occupied Germany

ITALY

Havel R.

Tegelersee *Tegel*

Berlin

Gatow *Spree R.*

Grosser Wannsee *Tempelhof* *Grosser Müggelsee*

• *Potsdam*

Schönefeld

American zone	
British zone	
French zone	
Soviet zone	
Airfield	
Air corridor	

0   100   200 mi.
0   100   200 km

ANDORRA

SPAIN

Mediterranean Sea

The airlift was restricted to flying within certain zones when delivering supplies.

The airlift generally ran smoothly, unless there was bad weather, which was often a problem. Tunner saw this for himself on August 13—"Black Friday." The general was aboard a C-54 that was part of a line of planes on their way to Tempelhof. Without warning, thick rain clouds dropped over

"SEEING" BY RADIO

During World War II, the British used a new technology for the first time. Called radio direction and ranging, or radar, it used radio waves to locate distant objects. At first the British used it to find enemy airplanes. Then radar was used by flight and naval crews to locate enemy targets. During the Berlin Airlift, a system called Ground Control Approach (GCA) used radar to help planes land in Berlin. With GCA, radar picked up the planes as they neared the airfields. Controllers on the ground used the radar to tell pilots how to turn as they approached the runway. Pilots were completely dependent on the GCA when it came to landing safely. GCA radar helped the airlift pilots fly day and night through all but the worst storms and fog.

the airport. Landing there was already difficult, because Tempelhof sat between many apartment buildings. Radar usually helped guide the pilots to the ground, but the heavy rain made the technology almost useless. One C-54 crashed into a ditch and erupted into flames. Another just barely missed running into the fire from the first crash. Planes waiting to land circled overhead, including Tunner's. He ordered all the planes except his to go back to their bases in western Germany.

He then made several key decisions for future airlift flights. All planes would fly the same route each time. Pilots would rely only on their instruments, rather than on what they could see. If a plane could not land for any reason at its scheduled time, it would return to base instead of wasting time in the air. U.S. troops called Tunner "Willie the Whip" because of his efforts to speed up delivery of the cargo. His skills made the Berlin Airlift more successful than ever. ◣

55

On the Ground

Chapter

6

Once in command of the Berlin Airlift, General Tunner made changes on the ground as well as in the air. He didn't want pilots leaving their planes to get food or water while the cargo was loaded and unloaded. Instead trucks carrying snacks began meeting the planes on the runways. Tunner also put in place strict rules for maintaining the aircraft to make sure there were always plenty in the air. Each plane was inspected daily and after every 50 hours, 200 hours, and 1,000 hours of flying.

Tunner had learned in Asia that keeping the crews in high spirits was key to a successful airlift. The troops in Germany sometimes grumbled as their tours of duty became longer than the 30 or 60 days they first thought they would serve. And some had to sleep in tents. Tunner tried

to improve small things to keep the crews happy. Dining halls were kept open so people could eat at any time. Doughnuts, hamburgers, and coffee were popular because they could be eaten on the go. Tunner also tried to improve mail service, and he began a newspaper, the *Task Force Times*, to keep everyone informed about the airlift. The paper featured cartoons to help tired crewmembers laugh at their uncomfortable surroundings.

A mechanic worked on a plane engine at an airfield in the British zone.

The airlift brought together Americans and Germans in increasing numbers. At the air bases, young German women ran the trucks that served food to the crewmembers flying into Berlin. The women greeted the hardworking pilots with smiles. A shortage of trained U.S. mechanics gave hundreds of skilled Germans a chance to work for the Americans, fixing the planes. Others with less skill did the loading and unloading of supplies. Their speedy work impressed at least one member of the U.S. Air Force, Victor Kregel. He later remembered, "It was just incredible. ... Whatever you had on board was whisked off. There was never any foot dragging."

The Germans played a key part in getting coal to Berlin. In the American and British sectors, barges carried coal to ports where German workers put it in bags. They then loaded the bags on trucks, which carried the coal to the air bases so it could

WOMEN IN BERLIN

Men weren't the only U.S. troops on the ground in Berlin. During World War II, the United States created the Women's Army Corps (WAC). Some WAC members remained in Europe when the war ended and served in Berlin. Just as the Berlin Airlift began, the U.S. government decided to make the WAC a permanent part of the military. Some U.S. lawmakers feared that if war broke out with the Soviet Union, not enough men would volunteer for the military. The lawmakers also did not want to start a draft, which would force men into the military. Having the WAC become permanent would help staff the Army during any Cold War conflict.

be brought to Berlin. A total of 1.5 million tons (1.35 million metric tons) of coal came to Berlin during the airlift—65 percent of the total cargo.

German workers also loaded and unloaded the various foods brought into Berlin. They included flour, potatoes, canned meat, and dried vegetables. Some fresh milk came in, but most was dehydrated—the water was removed. Without the water, the food weighed less, so more of it could be brought on each flight. Vegetables, potatoes, and eggs were also dehydrated. Not all the food was very tasty. German companies in the American and British sectors sent items they could not sell anywhere else. But most Germans welcomed what they received. They also got vitamin pills, since the food that reached Berlin was not enough to meet all their health needs.

Bags of coal and potatoes sat in trucks at an airfield, waiting to be loaded onto planes heading into Berlin.

Contact between the Western allies and Berliners reached a new level through the efforts of Lieutenant Gail Halvorsen, an American pilot. After meeting a group of Berlin children, Halvorsen told them he would drop candy for them from his plane. So they would know which plane was his, he would wiggle its wings up and down as he flew overhead. Halvorsen tied bundles of candy bars and gum to several tiny parachutes, then pushed them out of a chute used for emergency flares. The children got the candy, and soon the pilot came back with more. The young Berliners began calling Halvorsen the *Schokoladenflieger* (the "Chocolate Flyer") and *Onkel Wackelfluge* ("Uncle Wiggly Wings"). Americans soon knew him as the "Candy Bomber."

Packages of candy were prepared for the children of Berlin.

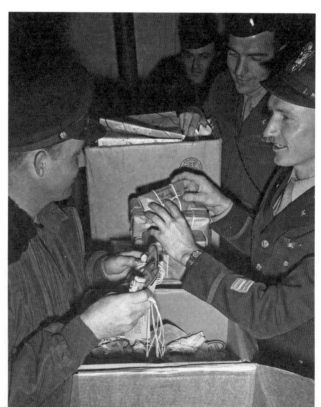

Halvorsen didn't tell his commanders about the candy "bombs," fearing they wouldn't approve. One officer found out when the story made the newspapers. He told Halvorsen, "You almost hit a German newspaperman on the head with a candy bar in Berlin yesterday, and he's got this story all over the world. The general read it and called me to find out what was going on." Instead of getting in trouble, Halvorsen won praise for promoting good relations with the Germans and showing the generosity of Americans.

OPERATION LITTLE VITTLES

Lieutenant Gail Halvorsen's candy bombings inspired others to help him bring chocolate to the children of Berlin. More pilots began dropping candy from their planes, and people in the United States began donating chocolate bars and the tiny pieces of cloth used as parachutes. Some American children gave money so the pilots could buy things for the children of Berlin, and a candy company donated candy. The dropping of candy from the planes was soon called Operation Little Vittles. When Halvorsen finished his service in Germany and returned to the United States, other pilots took over the program. In the end, 250,000 candy parachutes were dropped over Berlin.

The candy bars weren't the only "bombs" U.S. planes dropped over Berlin. Karin Kraus was lucky enough to catch a large balloon that drifted down toward the ground. Attached to it was a card informing her that she could trade the balloon for a package created by Cooperative for American Remittances to Europe (CARE). CARE packages were first sent to Europeans by more than 20 U.S. volunteer groups at the end of World War II. A smiling U.S. soldier handed Karin a 20-pound (nine-kilogram) package filled with food, including coffee, margarine, canned meat,

The continuous loading and unloading of supplies became a daily routine during the airlift.

and raisins. But Karin later remembered, "I was most interested in the chocolate, an entire pound of dark, rich chocolate."

Berliners continued to rely on the help of the United States and its allies because the Soviets refused to end the blockade. Stalin still wanted the Americans, British, and French to give up their plan to unite their zones. President Truman and the other leaders refused to meet the Soviet demand. To put on more pressure, the Soviets continued to disrupt meetings of the city council, which were held in their sector. At times, local communists hid canes and clubs in their pants legs to sneak the weapons into the meetings.

On September 9, rain fell as 300,000 people filled a city square to protest the blockade and Soviet attempts to control the city. Ernst Reuter said:

> *Today the people of Berlin will make their voice heard. People of America, England, France, Italy—look at this city. You cannot abandon this city and its people. You should not abandon it.*

After the rally, some German youths tore down a Soviet flag flying over a nearby gate. As the youths started to burn it, Soviet soldiers attacked them. One German was killed. Berliners saw once again that the Soviets were their enemies, and they were counting on the United States to help them keep their freedom.

Losses and Successes

With "Willie the Whip" Tunner in command, the Berlin Airlift ran like a well-oiled machine. At the Berlin airports, German crews worked faster and faster, cutting down the time needed to unload the planes, refuel them, and get them ready for their next flights. With this effort, the daily tonnage reached 5,000 tons (4,500 metric tons) by the end of September.

Planes landed or took off from Tempelhof and Gatow every 90 seconds. A plane flying west was nicknamed "Big Willie," and a plane flying east was called "Big Easy." The planes flew at about 170 miles (272 km) per hour at one of three different altitudes. At any given altitude, planes flew 15 minutes apart. They came into Berlin along the two outer air corridors

connecting the western sectors of the city with West Germany. On the return trip, the planes flew in the center corridor.

As more C-54s joined the airlift, U.S. officials and their allies decided to build a third airport in the French sector of Berlin. The large steamrollers and bulldozers needed for the construction were too big to fit inside the C-54s. The solution was to cut the equipment into smaller pieces, then weld them back together in Berlin. Once again, German civilians, especially women, collected bricks from destroyed buildings so they could be used to build runways. For their work, the people earned about one mark per hour and received one hot meal,

The British flew some cargo to Berlin in the Avro York, a transport version of a bomber plane they had used during World War II.

The first C-47 touched down at Tegel Airfield just three months after construction began.

usually a bowl of potato soup and a piece of black bread. With 17,000 Germans working in three shifts around the clock, Tegel Airfield opened in early November 1948.

The Western allies constantly made adjustments so they could bring more cargo into Berlin. The British introduced tanker planes that could carry diesel and other liquid fuel. Improved radar was brought in, and lights went up to help planes land in bad weather. As ice on the planes' wings became a problem, one U.S. sergeant came up with a solution. A large jet engine was attached to a truck. Turning on the engine created a blast of heat that melted the ice and dried the wings.

De-icing became important as the weather worsened in November and December. Because of the bad weather, the number of flights fell, and the daily tonnage plummeted. But by Christmas the weather had improved, and crews could come in with gifts for the citizens of Berlin. Some of the gifts were carried by Clarence the Camel.

ANOTHER "VITTLES"

Clarence the Camel wasn't the only animal to win fame during the airlift. While stationed in Germany, Lieutenant Russ Steber bought a boxer. He didn't have anyone to take care of the dog when he made flights into Berlin, so Steber took the dog with him. Named Vittles, the boxer flew on 131 flights with Steber and many more with other pilots. One day, Steber thought he was going to get in trouble when he was called in to see General Curtis LeMay. But LeMay just wanted to make sure Vittles was safe if Steber's plane ever crashed. He ordered the pilot to make a tiny parachute for the dog. The canine chute was tied to Steber's parachute, so if he ever left the plane, Vittles would come along with him. Pictures of Vittles appeared in newspapers all over the world. After the airlift, he traveled with Steber to the United States.

The weather was not the only problem. The Soviets tried to disrupt flights any way they could without directly attacking planes. They launched weather balloons near the air corridors and used special electronic devices to jam navigation systems. They sometimes fired guns near the planes without actually hitting them. Soviet fighter planes flew close by the C-54 Skymasters and other planes, hoping to startle the pilots. Gail Halvorsen later remembered:

> *We'd come up and have a Yak [Soviet fighter] come head on with you right nose to nose and at the last minute would peel off. Or come up behind you so you couldn't see him and then come up over the wing.*

Crewmembers also dealt with busy schedules that gave them little time to relax. Ford Garvin worked at an air base in the British zone. He worked shifts of 13 hours each, seven days a week, for six months without a single day off. To Garvin and others, the effort was worth it. They knew they were helping to keep more than 2 million people alive. To the Berliners on the ground, the never-ending stream of planes was a sign that the West had not forgotten them. One Berliner wrote, "We could shout with joy when at night the big birds fly back ... to get new supplies for Berlin."

Through the winter months, coal was in short supply. One Berlin woman produced small amounts of electricity by attaching a bicycle to a generator. People also learned to do some chores at midnight, when the power was on briefly.

Although the airlift brought in plenty of dried food, some Berliners craved fresh meat. Berlin resident Mercedes Wild remembered how her grandmother caught a sparrow that flew into their apartment. Mercedes was served a tiny piece of meat at lunch, but—thinking it was the sparrow—she could not eat it.

By January 15, 1949, the U.S. airlift fleet included nearly 250 C-54s, and the British had nearly 150. In January, the cargo reaching Berlin averaged 5,547 tons (4,992 metric tons) per day. Bad weather made the number drop slightly in February, but it increased again in March. In April, General Tunner decided he wanted "to do something to shake up the command," and "the answer was competition!" He would prod his crews to set a record for the most tonnage delivered in a single day. The day he picked was Easter Sunday.

The flights actually began at noon the day before, April 15, 1949. For 24 hours, the crews at the different bases worked faster than they ever had

DANGERS ON THE GROUND

One risk for U.S. pilots was mechanical problems. In September 1948, both engines on Captain Ken Slaker's plane lost power, and he had to parachute out before the plane crashed. He ended up in the Soviet zone, where he met Rudolph Schnabel. The friendly East German spoke some English and risked arrest to help Slaker cross back to the American zone. Slaker traveled with some East Germans who wanted to leave the Soviet zone. At one point, Slaker hurt his back, and the others pulled him up a hill, possibly saving his life. Slaker later repaid Schnabel for his aid by helping him and his wife escape from East Germany.

Totals for the Berlin Airlift	
Number of flights	277,569
Total amount of cargo	2.33 million tons (2.01 million metric tons)
Cargo delivered by Americans	1.78 million tons (1.6 million metric tons)
Cargo delivered by British	541,937 tons (487,743 metric tons)
Amount of coal	1.6 million tons (1.44 million metric tons)
Amount of food	536,000 tons (482,400 metric tons)

before. They knew they were trying to set a record. "Before long," Tunner wrote, "we were all caught up in the exuberance [excitement] of the mission." Tunner urged the men on by telling the crews at one base that those at another base were working even faster. When the Easter activity ended, 1,398 flights had brought almost 13,000 tons (11,700 metric tons) of coal into Berlin. The record-setting run was known as the Easter Parade. Tunner knew that the efforts that day "broke the back of the Berlin blockade."

Even before Easter, the Soviets had realized that the blockade would not force the Western allies to get rid of the B-marks or change their plans to create a new German state. In public comments, Stalin stopped bringing up the new currency, though earlier he had said that was the main reason for the blockade. U.S. officials took this as a sign that the Soviet leader might be softening about keeping the blockade in place. At almost the same time, in early February 1949, the United States and Great Britain tightened their counter-blockade into the Soviet zone.

Berliners watched as plane after plane landed at Tempelhof Airport.

71

Roadways as well as rails were now shut down. Several times during February and March, Philip Jessup, a U.S. delegate to the United Nations, met with the Soviet delegate, Jacob Malik. Jessup learned that Stalin was willing to talk about lifting the blockade. But he wanted a meeting of the heads of the four World War II Allies to discuss the future of Germany. At first, the Soviets wanted a promise that the other three victors would not create a new nation out of their German zones. Stalin then dropped this demand, realizing he could not stop the creation of a new, democratic German state. His blockade was not working, and he still was not ready to go to war over Germany.

On May 4, 1949, representatives from the four occupying nations met in New York. The Soviets agreed to remove all the restrictions on communications, transportation, and trade on May 12, 1949. The counter-blockade on East Berlin

THE TWO GERMANYS

For Germans in the western zones, May 12, 1949, was doubly important. As the blockade was ending in Berlin, the United States and its allies approved the creation of a new nation, the Federal Republic of Germany. Since the previous year, elected officials in the French, British, and U.S. zones had been working on the Basic Law. This document, similar to the Constitution in the United States, spelled out the rights of Germans and the workings of the government The new country was officially created on May 23, and it was commonly called West Germany. A few months later, the Soviet Union created the German Democratic Republic, or East Germany, in its zone.

and the Soviet zone would also end. In addition, all four countries agreed to meet in Paris on May 23 to discuss issues relating to Germany's future, including its currency.

The sight of trucks driving into their city cheered the weary residents of West Berlin. They would have fresh food again, and the power was soon back on. A teenager named Alice Sawadda rushed to a local café with her boyfriend to celebrate. They tried to stuff themselves with hot chocolate and cake, Alice recalled, "but we could not eat so much, because our bodies were not used to it." Karin Kraus went out to buy milk—"heavenly white, rich, liquid milk."

With the lifting of the blockade on May 12, 1949, Berliners lined the streets to welcome the first trucks bringing food into the city.

CARE packages, containing food, soap, and other daily needs, continued to enter Berlin after the lifting of the blockade.

The end of the blockade did not end the airlift. General Clay wanted to bring in just over 1 million tons (900,000 metric tons) of coal and food, in case of future troubles in Berlin. Planes operated by the United States and its allies continued to fly until September 30, 1949. General Tunner felt sure that

he could get the airlift running again in hours if the Western allies ever needed it. The airlift had shown the ability of British and American crews to keep a city alive.

The efforts that Germans had made during the airlift won the respect of many Americans, including General Clay. "The determination of the people did not falter [weaken]," Clay wrote. "They had earned their right to freedom." The Berlin Airlift also showed the democratic countries of Europe—and Joseph Stalin—that the United States was determined to contain communism wherever it could. ◣

After the Blockade

The United States and its allies remained busy throughout the airlift. They officially united their zones and formed West Germany. Its capital was Bonn, a city on the Rhine River in the British zone. With the creation of this new German nation, the Americans, the British, and the French gave up political control over their former zones. Their troops, however, remained in West Germany.

During the same time, the Western allies recruited nine other nations to join the North Atlantic Treaty Organization (NATO). The group was organized to keep the Soviets from launching a new war in Europe. The members of NATO agreed that an armed attack against one or more of the member countries would be considered an attack against them all.

Much of the city of Bonn, Germany's new capital, had to be rebuilt after World War II.

NATO THEN AND NOW

The North Atlantic Treaty Organization (NATO) was created on April 4, 1949. In addition to the three countries that occupied West Berlin, its members were Italy, Canada, Belgium, Luxembourg, Iceland, Norway, Portugal, Denmark, and the Netherlands. Greece and Turkey joined in 1952, West Germany was added in 1955, and Spain joined in 1982. After the end of the Cold War in 1991, 10 nations once under Soviet control also became part of NATO. Russia is considered a partner, though not an official member. Today NATO protects the security and freedom of its members. Since 2003, troops from NATO nations have served in Afghanistan as part of the war on terror.

Lucius Clay returned to West Berlin in October 1950 as the city continued to slowly rebuild. He presented the city with a copy of the Liberty Bell. This symbol of American freedom is on display in Philadelphia. The copy, called the Freedom Bell, was hung in a tower in West Berlin. Clay also presented the names of 1 million people from across the United States who had promised to resist communism in any way they could. Almost 500,000 Berliners came out to greet Clay, and city leaders renamed a local street for him.

With the end of the blockade, the United States and its allies had won the first major struggle of the Cold War. They had kept West Berlin free and showed Stalin they would not give in to his demands. West Berliners, and people all across Western Europe, saw that the United States was serious about defending democracy. Stalin learned

CRUSADE FOR FREEDOM

this, too, though he and future Soviet leaders would continue to try to spread communism wherever they could.

In 1951, the city of Berlin opened the Luftbrucke Memorial at Tempelhof to honor those who had participated in the airlift. The memorial represents a broken bridge, and its three tall bands stand for the three air corridors that linked Berlin to the West. Berliners call the concrete statue *die Gabel*, meaning "the fork," or *die Hunger-Harke*, meaning "the hunger rake."

A matching memorial stands outside the airport at the Rhein-Main air base near Frankfurt. Seventy-seven people died during the airlift,

Young Berliners circled the Freedom Bell, which arrived in Berlin in October 1950. The bell was a symbol of the desire for freedom shared by Americans and Berliners during and after the airlift.

The Luftbrucke (Air Bridge) Memorial at Tempelhof Airport was erected to honor the military men and civilians who died during the airlift.

including 31 Americans. The dead included both soldiers and civilians. Carved into the Berlin memorial are the names of the American and British troops killed and German words that mean "They gave their lives for the freedom of Berlin serving in the Airlift 1948/49."

With the four occupied zones of Germany divided into two countries, East Berlin served as the capital of East Germany, while West Berlin was just a small island of freedom in the middle of a communist nation. But thanks to the Marshall Plan and other aid, that half of the city was rebuilding quickly. East Berlin, however, became a bleak place. One East Berlin construction worker described life in his city during the early 1950s:

> *The average person lived very badly. If you're talking about the things everybody needs like heating, coal, electricity, these things were all rationed. Electricity for domestic use was simply not available. The morale of the population dropped to zero.*

As East Germans realized they were doomed to live under communism, thousands of them began to come to East Berlin. From there, they would cross over to the western half of the city, seeking jobs and freedom. Some kept on moving, settling in West Germany or other countries.

In 1961, East German leader Walter Ulbricht took drastic action to stop the flow of East Germans to the West. He asked the Soviet Union for permission to build a barrier between East Berlin and West Berlin. The Soviets let him first build a wire fence, which went up on the night of August 13, 1961. When the Western allies did not protest or try to stop the East Germans, Ulbricht put up a permanent concrete wall.

U.S. leaders did not take action against the wall because they did not want a "hot" war in Berlin. Their main concern was keeping West Berlin free and democratic. The Berlin Wall made life hard for many West Berliners who had friends or relatives on the other side. But the wall did not weaken their freedom. For East Germans, however, the wall was a solid sign of what their communist leaders would do to control their lives.

In July 1962, almost one year after the first barbed-wire fence divided East and West Berlin, a much stronger concrete wall was erected past the Brandenburg Gate, near the border of the two halves of the city.

For almost 30 years, the Berlin Wall separated East Berlin and West Berlin. The East Germans built taller walls and placed armed guards all along it. They added new barriers between the city and the wall. Even so, approximately 5,000 people managed to escape by climbing over the wire fence, hiding in cars, or tunneling under the wall. Two families even built their own hot-air balloon and flew from East Germany to the West. At least 133 people and possibly as many as 1,245—were killed trying to escape, and thousands were caught and thrown in jail.

In 1989, life changed again in East Germany and in other European nations under Soviet control. The Soviet leader Mikhail Gorbachev was giving these nations greater freedom. People held protests and called for the end of communist rule. By October 1989, hundreds of thousands of East Germans were filling the streets of Leipzig and other cities. They too demanded freedom. The East German government then replaced Erich Hoeneker, a strict communist, with Egon Krenz, who saw the need for reform. He ordered the opening of East Germany's borders so people could travel freely. On November 9, East Berliners began to cross into West Berlin. The Berlin Wall was now open.

In March 1990, East Germany held its first free elections in more than 40 years. Voters eliminated the communists from the East German government. In Germany, at least, the Cold War was over. Berlin was united, and soon East Germany and West Germany were as well.

THE BERLIN AIRLIFT

East and West Berliners celebrated the opening of the Berlin Wall, ending 28 years of separation in their city.

With the end of the Cold War, some Germans thought back to the days of the airlift. Etza Reuter, the son of Berlin mayor Ernst Reuter, spoke about what the airlift meant to Berliners:

There was a growing feeling that the Germans, after all, can be satisfied to accept democracy as their own ways of living and to become part of the western world. And that was what really went on during the blockade, together with the airlift, together with ... those courageous young chaps flying those—those airplanes into Berlin ... everything came together, after all it was a very, very positive experience."

Working together, the United States and its allies, along with the determined people of Berlin, stood up to the Soviet Union and saved a city from starvation.

Timeline

September 1, 1939

Germany invades Poland, beginning World War II.

June 22, 1941

Germany invades the Soviet Union.

December 7, 1941

Japan attacks Pearl Harbor, Hawaii, bringing the United States into World War II.

June 6, 1944

 D-Day begins the Allied invasion of France and the effort to push the Germans out of Western Europe.

August 2, 1944

The Big Three powers of Great Britain, the United States, and the Soviet Union agree to divide Germany into three zones and jointly occupy Berlin.

February 4–11, 1945

The Big Three meet in Yalta and agree to create a fourth zone in Germany for France to occupy.

April 20, 1945

Soviet troops begin a major assault of Berlin.

May 8, 1945

World War II in Europe ends.

July 3, 1945

U.S. troops take control of the American sector of Berlin.

July 17–August 2, 1945

 At Potsdam, Allied leaders make their final plans for the division of Germany.

November 30, 1945

The Allied Control Council creates three air corridors linking Berlin with the American and British zones.

February 7, 1946

Radio in the American Sector (RIAS) begins broadcasting in Berlin.

March 12, 1947

U.S. President Harry S. Truman outlines the Truman Doctrine to fight the spread of communism in Europe.

December 19, 1947

Truman asks Congress to begin funding the Marshall Plan to aid Europe.

March 20, 1948

Soviet military officers walk out of a meeting of the Allied Control Council.

April 1, 1948

The Soviets begin to restrict travel into the western sectors of Berlin.

April 2, 1948

General Lucius Clay puts General Curtis LeMay in charge of an airlift to bring supplies to U.S. troops.

April 5, 1948

A Soviet fighter plane collides with a British plane, killing 14 people.

June 18, 1948

The Allies announce plans to introduce new currency in their zones of Germany.

June 19, 1948

All passenger train service into West Berlin is halted.

June 23, 1948

Berlin city council votes to use the Allies' currency in West Berlin and a new Soviet currency in East Berlin.

June 24, 1948

The Soviet Union begins a complete blockade of West Berlin.

June 26, 1948

 Planes operated by the United States and its allies begin the Berlin Airlift, bringing 80 tons (72 metric tons) of cargo.

July 18, 1948

Gail Halvorsen drops his first "candy bombs" over Berlin.

July 28, 1948

General William Tunner arrives in Berlin to run the airlift for the United States and its allies.

August 5, 1948

 German civilians begin building a new airport, Tegel, in the French sector of Berlin.

August 13, 1948

Bad weather prevents many planes from landing in Berlin, and Tunner introduces new policies designed to increase the number of planes that reach the city.

September 6, 1948

Communist mobs attack city council members meeting in the Soviet sector of Berlin.

September 9, 1948

300,000 Berliners attend a rally to protest the blockade and call for continued aid from the United States and its allies.

September 18, 1948

U.S. and British planes deliver 6,988 tons (6,289 metric tons) of supplies to Berlin, a daily record at that time.

November 5, 1948

Construction of Tegel Airfield is complete.

Timeline

November 9, 1948

U.S. Air Force reports it has 258 C-54s assigned to Operation Vittles, but only 169 are actually able to fly. Average daily tonnage for that months is 3,407 tons (2,765 metric tons).

December 26, 1948

On the six-month anniversary of the Berlin Airlift, planes bring in more than 6,000 tons (5,400 metric tons) of supplies.

April 4, 1949

The United States and 11 other countries form the North Atlantic Treaty Organization (NATO).

April 15, 1949

The "Easter Parade" begins, which sets a one-day tonnage record for the airlift.

May 4, 1949

The Soviet Union agrees to end the blockade of West Berlin.

May 12, 1949

Soviets officially end the blockade; the United States and its allies approve the creation of West Germany.

May 23, 1949

The Federal Republic of Germany (West Germany) is officially created.

September 30, 1949

Last airlift flight leaves for Berlin.

October 7, 1949

The German Democratic Republic (East Germany) is created.

October 24, 1950

General Clay presents the Freedom Bell to the people of West Berlin.

August 13, 1961

East German soldiers and police officers begin shutting down checkpoints between East Berlin and West Berlin and erecting a barbed-wire fence between the two halves of the city.

October 9, 1989

70,000 East Germans gather in Leipzig to protest communist rule in their country.

November 9, 1989

East German officials open the Berlin Wall, allowing their citizens free access to West Berlin.

October 3, 1990

East and West Germany unite.

ON THE WEB

For more information on this topic, use FactHound.

1 Go to *www.facthound.com*

2 Type in this book ID: 0756534860

3 Click on the *Fetch It* button. FactHound will find the best Web sites for you.

HISTORIC SITES

National Museum of the United States Air Force
1100 Spaatz St.
Wright-Patterson AFB, OH 45433-7102
937/255-3284

The museum features an exhibit on the Berlin Airlift.

Berlin Airlift Historical Foundation
P.O. Box 782
Farmingdale, NJ 07727
732/818-0034

Visit the *Spirit of Freedom*, a restored Douglas C-54E transport aircraft, which can be seen at events scheduled throughout the year.

LOOK FOR MORE BOOKS IN THIS SERIES

Black Tuesday:
Prelude to the Great Depression

The Cultural Revolution:
Years of Chaos in China

A Day Without Immigrants:
Rallying Behind America's Newcomers

The Iran-Contra Affair:
Political Scandal Uncovered

Kristallnacht, The Night of Broken Glass:
Igniting the Nazi War Against Jews

The March on Washington:
Uniting Against Racism

A complete list of **Snapshots in History** titles is available on our Web site: *www.compasspointbooks.com*

Glossary

Allied Control Council
body created after World War II by the United States, the Soviet Union, Great Britain, and France to deal with matters relating to Germany

allies
friends or helpers; when capitalized, refers to the United States and its allies during major wars

blockade
military effort to keep goods from entering and leaving a region

capitalist
supporter of capitalism, an economic system that allows people to freely create businesses and own as much property as they can afford

communist
country or person practicing communism, a political system in which there is no private property and everything is owned and shared in common

deutsche mark
unit of currency used in western Germany starting in 1948

European Advisory Commission
body created during World War II by the United States, the Soviet Union, and Great Britain to make plans for dealing with Germany after the war

Kommandatura
council created by the United States, the Soviet Union, Great Britain, and France to govern Berlin

Marshall Plan
U.S. effort named for Secretary of State George Marshall to send aid to Europe

occupation
the continued presence of the victors in the country they have defeated, to run the government and restore order

propaganda
information or ideas, some true and some untrue, that are deliberately spread among the public to try to influence its thinking

reparations
payments made to make amends for wrongdoing

Sozialistische Einheitspartei Deutschlands (SED)
German for Socialist Unity Party, the Communist Party the Soviet Union created in its zone of Germany

Trummerfrauen
German for rubble women, the German women who helped clear the bricks from destroyed buildings in Berlin

Source Notes

Chapter 1

Page 10, lines 12 and 14: William H. Tunner. *Over the Hump*. Washington, D.C.: Office of the Air Force Historian, 1985, p. 194. 22 May 2007. www.airforcehistory. hq.af.mil/Publications/fulltext/over_the_hump.pdf

Page 11, line 1: Karin Finell. *Goodbye to the Mermaids: A Childhood Lost in Hitler's Berlin*. Columbia: University of Missouri Press, 2006, p. 275.

Page 13, line 5: Stewart M. Powell. "The Berlin Airlift." *Journal of the Air Force Association*, June 1998. 20 May 2007. www.afa.org/magazine/June1998/0698 berlin.asp

Page 13, sidebar line 9: Richard Corliss. "That Old Feeling: A Berlin Biopic." *Time*. 25 May 2007. www.time.com/time/sampler/article/0,8599,190220,00.html

Page 13, sidebar line 16: *CNN Cold War*. Episode 4: Berlin. 19 May 2007. www.cnn.com/SPECIALS/cold.war/episodes/04/script.html

Page 15, sidebar: Thomas Parrish. *Berlin in the Balance, 1945–1949*. Reading, Mass.: Perseus Books, 1998, p. 257.

Page 15, line 7: Ibid., p. 300.

Chapter 2

Page 20, line 6: Franklin D. Roosevelt Library and Museum. German Diplomatic Files, Box 31. 24 April 2007. www.fdrlibrary.marist.edu/psf/box31/t297c05.html

Page 22, line 1: *Berlin in the Balance, 1945–1949*, p. 85.

Chapter 3

Page 25, line 2: *Goodbye to the Mermaids: A Childhood Lost in Hitler's Berlin*, p.160.

Page 26, line 6: Robert P. Grathwol and Donita M. Moorhus. *Berlin and the American Military: A Cold War Chronicle*. New York: New York University Press, 1999, p. 9.

Page 27, line 3: *Goodbye to the Mermaids: A Childhood Lost in Hitler's Berlin,* p.160.

Page 27, line 9: *Berlin in the Balance, 1945–1949*, p. 29.

Page 28, line 11: *CNN Cold War*.

Page 29, line 12: Frank Howley. *Berlin Command*. New York: G.P. Putnam's Sons, 1950, p. 80.

Page 31, line 4: *Berlin and the American Military: A Cold War Chronicle*, p. 30.

Page 33, sidebar: *CNN Cold War*.

Page 34, line 12: *Goodbye to the Mermaids: A Childhood Lost in Hitler's Berlin*, p. 233.

Chapter 4

Page 39, line 12: *Berlin in the Balance, 1945–1949*, p. 151.

Page 41, sidebar: *Over the Hump*, p. 165.

Source Notes

Page 42, line 19: *Berlin in the Balance, 1945–1949*, p. 151.

Page 43, line 26: *Goodbye to the Mermaids: A Childhood Lost in Hitler's Berlin,* p. 257.

Page 44, line 6: *Berlin in the Balance, 1945–1949*, p. 166.

Page 45, line 4: *CNN Cold War.*

Chapter 5
Page 48, lines 14 and 19: John H. Backer. *Winds of History: The German Years of Lucius DuBignon Clay.* New York: Van Nostrand Reinhold Company, 1983, pp. 498 and 236.

Page 49, line 15: *CNN Cold War.*

Page 51, line 27: Ibid.

Page 53, line 13: *Over the Hump,* p. 162.

Chapter 6
Page 58, line 12: "The Berlin Airlift."

Page 61, line 7: *CNN Cold War.*

Page 62, line 1: *Goodbye to the Mermaids: A Childhood Lost in Hitler's Berlin,* p. 270.

Page 63, line 4: *CNN Cold War.*

Chapter 7
Page 68, line 11: Ibid.

Page 68, line 25: *Berlin in the Balance, 1945–1949*, p. 227.

Page 69, line 23: *Over the Hump,* pp. 219.

Page 70, lines 2 and 10: Ibid., pp. 220 and 222.

Page 73, line 11: *Berlin in the Balance, 1945–1949*, p. 325.

Page 73, line 13: *Goodbye to the Mermaids: A Childhood Lost in Hitler's Berlin,* p. 282.

Page 75, line 7: Roger Miller. *To Save a City: The Berlin Airlift*, 1948–1949. Washington, D.C.: U.S. Government Printing Office, 1998, p. 112.

Chapter 8
Page 80, line 4: "Airlift Landmarks." *The German Way & More.* 25 May 2007. www.german-way.com/alfoto02.html

Page 81, line 11: *CNN Cold War.* Episode 7: After Stalin. 25 May 2007. www.cnn.com/SPECIALS/cold.war/episodes/07/script.html

Page 85, line 1: National Security Archive. *CNN Cold War* Interviews. 25 May, 2007. www.gwu.edu/~nsarchiv/coldwar/interviews/episode-4/reuter4.html

SELECT BIBLIOGRAPHY

Backer, John H. *Winds of History: The German Years of Lucius DuBignon Clay.* New York: Van Nostrand Reinhold Company, 1983.

Finell, Karin. *Goodbye to the Mermaids: A Childhood Lost in Hitler's Berlin.* Columbia: University of Missouri Press, 2006.

Grathwol, Robert P., and Donita M. Moorhus. *Berlin and the American Military: A Cold War Chronicle.* New York: New York University Press, 1999.

Howley, Frank. *Berlin Command.* New York: G.P. Putnam's Sons, 1950.

Isaacs, Jeremy, and Taylor Downing. *Cold War: An Illustrated History, 1945–1991.* New York: Little, Brown and Company, 1998.

Parrish, Thomas. *Berlin in the Balance, 1945–1949.* Reading, Mass: Perseus Books, 1998.

Paterson, Thomas G., J. Garry Clifford, and Kenneth J. Hagan. *American Foreign Relations: A History Since 1895.* Boston: Houghton Mifflin, 2000.

Willmott, H.P., et al. *World War II.* New York: DK Publishing, 2004.

FURTHER READING

Brager, Bruce L. *The Iron Curtain: The Cold War in Europe.* Philadelphia: Chelsea House, 2004.

Irwin, David W., Jr. *Highway to Freedom: The Berlin Airlift.* Paducah, Ky.: Turner Publishing Company, 2002.

Matthews, John R. *The Rise and Fall of the Soviet Union.* San Diego: Lucent Books, 2000.

Otfinoski, Steven. *Harry S. Truman: America's 33rd President.* Danbury, Conn.: Children's Press, 2005.

Westerfield, Scott. *The Berlin Airlift.* Englewood Cliffs, N.J.: Silver Burdett Press, 1989.

Index

ABOUT THE AUTHOR

Michael Burgan is a freelance writer for both children and adults. A graduate of the University of Connecticut with a degree in history, he has written more than 100 fiction and nonfiction books for children. He specializes in U.S. history. Michael has also written news articles, essays, and plays. He is a recipient of an Educational Press Association of America award.

IMAGE CREDITS

Associated Press **cover**, akg-images pp. **6** and **60**, **14** (Tony Vaccaro), **20** and **86** (Hulton Archive), **2** and **53** and **87**, **5** and **59**, **17**, **40**, **45**, **57**, **back cover (middle)** and **62**, **65** and **88**, **80**; Corbis pp. **11**, **12**, **30**, **39**, **back cover (left)** and **49**, **50**, **66** and **87**, **71**, **74**, **79**, **82** (Bettmann), **47** (Hulton-Deutsch Collection), **84** and **88** (Régis Bossu/Sygma), **22**; Getty **back cover (right)** and pp. **9**, **28**, **73** (Hulton Archive), **77** (Walter Sanders/Time Life Pictures).